To: J...

Brilliant heart
Brilliant words

Love
you are
#Necessary

73

The Heart of a Comet

ೞ

by Pages D. Matam

Write Bloody Publishing
America's Independent Press

Austin, TX

WRITEBLOODY.COM

The Heart of a Comet

© 2014 Write Bloody Publishing
No part of this book may be used or performed without written consent from the author, except for critical articles or reviews.

Write Bloody
First Edition
ISBN: 9781938912498

Cover art by Ashley Siebels
Proofread by Melinda Aguilar, Alex Kryger, B. Sharise Moore, and Terisa Siagatonu
Edited by Alex Kryger, B. Sharise Moore, and Terisa Siagatonu
Interior layout by Ashley Siebels
Author photo by Yveka Pierre

Type set in Bergamo from www.theleagueofmoveabletype.com

Printed in Tennessee, USA

Write Bloody Publishing
Austin, TX
Support Independent Presses
writebloody.com

To contact the author, send an email to writebloody@gmail.com

MADE IN THE USA

*The precise role of the artist, then, is to illuminate that darkness
blaze roads through that vast forest, so that we will not,
in all our doing, lose sight of its purpose, which is, after all,
to make the world a more human dwelling place.*

—James Baldwin, "The Creative Process"

THE HEART OF A COMET

A JOURNEY OF PURPOSE

THE HEART OF A COMET
A JOURNEY OF PURPOSE

SECOND WIND AND A SPOONFUL OF SUGAR

DUST TRAIL SUBJECTS

HUMANCATCHER'S COMA

Precursor to a fall (foreword)

You could say that this book has been almost three years in the making. But in fact, Comet has been a life time in the making. His story is mine just as much as it is yours in all of its conceptual miscellany of heaven, hell, and earth at all of its most sacred intersections.

This would mean that this book in fact is more so Comet's creation, not my own. I am only a vessel trying to portray the energy which he emits. The cosmic tail which follows the moment of kinesis. I've burned through too many life experiences at my soul's expense, and the ash buildup was becoming such a stain on every part of me that I wished to see grow. I had burned every bridge to myself, and thus didn't know how to connect to the world outside anymore. Lost in space, addicted to the escape, trying desperately to keep up appearances on the surface.

To think only a nickel and a decade ago, I barely spoke English. That I emigrated from a country that has known its fair share of troubles often sending generations on a search for milk and honey in far-off lands with nothing but pride and hope clutched between their teeth. The push and pull of "family" was a tug of war I usually found myself on the losing side of. Love and relationships (romantic and/or familial) were becoming constellations I could only dream of touching. But somehow through some brilliantly stitched fabric of the universe, I have been gifted with the only thing in my life that finally...fits. And it isn't poetry, or music, or any of my artistic talents and endeavors. But I was finally able to acquire a space within it all to love myself in the most holistic and holiest of manners. Have you ever offered yourself back to yourself, grabbed your heart and soul with your own two hands and marveled at such a beautiful construction? wondered why you have neglected you for so long and what was it that made you commit to such a reckless decision in the first place?

This book represents my first genuine attempt and follow-through with self care. It isn't my escape but a coming out party. A self-reflective process in which I am analyzing and taking responsibility for all of my actions. It is love hijacking all of my passions, my dreams, my goals, my very essence, until I can't help but can't help but burst into all of its gentle flames. This fire is elevated by the wind of every person who picks up this book. You are just as much a part of its making: from its spark to its conflagration, spreading across each individual cosmos that makes up a part of this universe. This book is a rapid oxidation of a paramount step towards radical self love. An intricate but necessary part to all journeys of discovery and purpose.

So in turn, to the person reading this...

...IN THE NAME OF LOVE, I DEDICATE THIS TO YOU.

THE APOLOGY OF A
CONFUSED TORNADO

PT. I

EYALA (THE CONFLICTS IN LEARNING HOW TO UN-BREAK)

I. Man vs. Himself

When you wake up drenched in tomorrow's amnesia,
your pulse still burning filled with troubling memories
grab the nearest item made of glass
and throw it to the wall... rip up clothes...break some furnitures...
cut yourself along the way. do something ANYTHING

...that reminds you, you are still human. That your heart is not a dandelion,so you must stop scattering yourself to pieces at the mercy of someone else's breath.

Stop falling in love with others more than your own reflection,
as the only way to exist. live in your skin
eyala is to look at yourself even in the dark of you
How ugly must we be rendered in order to be called
by everyone else beauty.

II. Man vs. Society

This is for the days
When eyala is poetry, becoming reconstructive surgery for the gaping spirit.
When prayers go where hands can't.
When my black is the color of bull's eye and my name snaps trigger.
When I will have to hold my children like bullet wounds.
When I will have to unlearn how to hate myself.
When America's favorite song will dance my flesh into illusion.
When the beat just will not go on.
There will be many.
You'll feel beaten down by the weight of your own galaxy,
The shooting star emptying its clip into the sky on a celestial drive-by;
But if we are going to live on the shoulders of giants,
We will have to stop complaining of our fear of heights.

III. Man vs. Nature

Something about the way you can see the universe ripping itself apart
in the grieving voice of a man shattering. Because he has to. Better
him than the world. But the world be he. All encompassing. His heart
be as tall as the sky. Spirit magnified to the unquenched depth of oceans.
Soulquariums that stretch for miles into the infinite of space. But how
many times must we destroy the star inside of us to give birth to someone
else's universe? You cannot supernova your way into someone else's heart.
A smile is eyala. All of your dreams buried in your last true love's kiss dipped
in a cosmos of sweat, moonlit regrets, and all but the last drop of
your combustible devotion.

IV. Man vs. God
We are all God's workmanship:
Our breath be ink, our flesh be paper. But even as often

As He writes, I swear looking
At my life, I am the reason God no longer believes in trees.

There is so much gravity
Hidden inside of us. So many psalms hidden inside of us.

Secrets we hold as we
persevere in our journeys at trying to find love, or ourselves,

Or joy. Or God. Whatever
She may be. Thought I found her at the altar of your spine.

You said you knew all too well
of the lies I hide beneath skies when closets grew up too quickly.

I told you I was leaving,
but you knew I'd come back running

with hands holding every scar
I forgot to leave behind. My palms wish for eyala.

V. Man vs. (Wo)Man

She's that kind of woman.
Always stepping out of a dream, dripping wet in marvelous,
Keeps shotguns tucked in the hems of her skirt,
Hides grenades under her freshly painted nails,
And keeps booby traps between her teeth.
Watch how you kiss her...
it better be with sincerity and intentions to stay.
Even her smile can seduce the grim reaper to suicide,
A woman who curses like Delilah's scissors,
Holding hands with razors but never seems to bleed.
None of her wounds are visible.
They are all lying somewhere lonely in a pile of regrets,
impatient as the truth, waiting to be picked up by a man
With hands way too big for his own pride...eyala.

A CANCEROUS GROWTH:
FROM ASHES TO ASHES

When my five year old son asked me,
     what did you want to be when you grew up?
I immediately shifted to a time in middle school
when a teacher asked this daunting question.

Ever since I was eight years old, I've wanted to grow up to become a cigarette
because it was the only thing that my father could never abandon.

For as long as I can remember,
I always felt like a man constantly in reverse,
like the backwash of a dream,
like karma's favorite crash test dummy,
constantly begging someone for all the love they have already given me.

I started drinking and being with women
in order to fill up the potholes inside my spirit.
But drinking more Absolut only made me more obsolete.
Now, I'm just a soul made out of 50% recycled plastic,
An assembly of a man, who loves like a runaway locomotive.
I treated the bodies of women
like mirrors because the more orgasms I gave them,
the more beautiful I became in my eyes.

When I was 13, I started building
train tracks— on my stomach,
some on thighs—
to all the parts of me I wished I could forget.
But that only made me more of a swollen dirty pile of remorse,
with a fiendish appetite for earthquakes at the dripping enjambment of a woman—
the earth shifts between my teeth and usually never returns the same;
misshapen planets have always tasted better to me.
But there is no gravity to my will;
all I'm left with is this vulgar smile stitched to a sense of humor
hiding the boy with the skin of a scarecrow
because it's the only way his corny heart can ward off the birds and the bees.

The only thing my father ever passed on to me
is this uncanny ability to hurt the people we love the most:
in a split second, I lost a woman that I thought I loved
more than my third-degree scars.
The very next year on a random doctor's visit,
I found out that I was alcohol intolerant.
I've drunk so much over the years that liquor
has become poisonous to my blood,
so my very next shot could have very well been my last.
You know, God has a funny sense of humor—
took away the two things I harbored the most
to teach me of real love, to teach me that liquor and women
are not a cure to my loneliness.

So what do you want to be when you grow up?

Honestly, I've always wanted to be a pediatrician,
one that helps save and heal children
starting with the one within myself.

Who would've known
in the 15 years it took to write this poem
that I would grow up to become a pediatrician,
making a stethoscope out of a microphone,
writing poems like daily prescriptions, and turning the stage
into a patient room for the healing of me to start within.
When you are on the search for the divine inside yourself,
you are often lead to the harsh realization
that you've been more Rick James than First James
with built-in fire escapes inside of your bones.

So what kind of legacy would I pass on to my son?
A legacy of burnt out men with hands like ashtrays
for him to inherit all of the butts of my mistakes?

I used to want to grow up to become a cigarette
     made sense because *I'm a Cancer,*
but there is no chemotherapy to my astronomy.

Yet, I still radiate like a sun afraid to shine
but always willing to give all of his light
to save anyone's sunset.
Which is all but the excruciating reality
That I do not want to die alone.

Son:
you can grow up to be anything that you want
but you are so much more than a cigarette,
more than just an excuse with a slow burning pulse
because if you ever heart the escape,
it will only have you falling in love with your own, cancerous growth.

GENESIS ACCORDING TO HIP-HOP

in 7 tankas

In the beginning
there was Hip-Hop. Hip-Hop was
with God. Hip-Hop was
God scratching light from darkness,
calling it the perfect mix.

The break was born from
asphalt skies and cardboard clouds.
Shell Tops pumped freshest
Gillespie contortionists—
Dizzy wind, bebop backspins.

Calligraphy of
spray cans growing more alive,
planting images
like gardens on trains, colored
vines from concrete sea of walls.

The starlight of beats
bellowing from cratered moon
inside of your throat.
Changing rhythms like seasons,
suns with hearts like eight-oh-eight.

Echo of gunshots
slithering in the emcee's
crafty tongue. Macho
creatures. No one can take your
fly. Microphone animal.

The lions would roar
Louder Than A Bomb. The GOATs
would prosper from their
36 chambers. Gold rope
wraps fist to protect rib with.

And on seventh day,
Blessed and Holy in its make,
Hip-Hop was sovereign.
Let all trumpets flare marvel;
praise the planet of Brooklyn.

FOR MY SOL

The theory of quantum entanglement states, "If two electrons are created together, they are forever entangled....Regardless of the distance between the two electrons, a change in quantum spin in one electron will immediately cause the other electron to change spin as well. In theory, you could separate two electrons by as much space as you wanted (say, the breadth of the universe), and they'd still be linked in such a way that actions taken on one would affect the other instantaneously. The theory has not been disproven; no one can prove such an invisible force does not exist."

It has been awhile since Comet has seen Sol. The last time they saw each other was at the start of his untimely fall. Sol was still much younger then, unable to truly comprehend his frail and innocent hand in such a gentle matter, unable to comprehend how his gravity would pull Comet back.

Sol had always been mischievous, with limitless imagination. He is still learning, growing, watching Comet's every move...even from a distance. He knows he ignites him every time they are close. He articulates it in smiles and silly laughter. Sol knows Comet understands him; they are just entangled that way.

But that's just it: their connection has become the very thing driving them apart. When you fall prey to circumstance, are you still ruled by destiny or fate? Comet knows that wherever they may be, they will always be linked by some invisible force or energy, the very same one that brought them together in the first place. Such a concept is still foreign to Sol, but Comet has made his resolve inextinguishable. He carefully crafts everyaction, knowing that they will affect Sol, no matter how much space there may be between them.

The obstacle that remains: how can he teach Sol not to be afraid to fall out of the sky or encourage him to burn as brightly as he possibly can when the time arises? How can he teach him that he matters and that with only a breadth of the universe away from Sol, nothing can take this from him?

Not even me.

YOU DO NOT BEAR MY LAST NAME

and my blood does not ring
in your veins. The only background
we share is of fathers who never came
back to ground us.

Your mother gave you the last name Jackson
after your great-grandfather, a bricklayer.
Your last name means foundation;
your last name is a means for construction.
People will teach you how to destroy
before ever showing you how to build.

I never took to the title of stepfather,
only took to stepping up to the plate.
After being dined on and skipped out
on the bill of fatherhood,
your birth was a reluctant chore
your father would not inherit.

My last name—Matam—means "ball;"
my last name is bravery
or a tool for games—
how my ancestors hid such meaning
as if they knew my father would never have
the balls to play his part.
  ...I inherited my father's inadequacy.

We are our mothers' greatest poems.
Our fathers were the crossed out lines,
the painful edit, the unnecessary word
everyone will need context clues
to discover its meaning. How did their meanings
help to further define us—
bravery,
foundation,
  dirty dish?

My father gave me O type blood,
a reluctant inheritance.
I hold the world in my veins just as strongly as I do
a lifetime of questions,
a history of addiction,
and of treating women like tools for games.

There were nights I held you
like the attempt to right my
father's wrongs, like the right choice,
like a proud last name.

As the father to you I learned to be...
these are my most sacred rules of living:

*(In lieu of emergency, break this from
the glass case of your heart.
Use its contents like an axe to
break free from reckless decisions)*

1. Bear hugs will become more bear traps
in a forest of unkept promises.
Do not turn a lover into prey for feast;
your name is not a hunter. You are not a dirty dish.

2. Understand that you are only as strong
as the women that stand by you.
Their love can easily be blueprint or wolf's howl.
Your name is foundation.

3. Making love is stepping on a landmine...
promising with heartbeats
to never lift your feet until you truly understand
the meaning of exploding into one another.

4. You are beautiful, black boy,
I love you, black boy,
you are beautiful, black boy,
your name is bravery.

Would Joseph still be a man
if he had decided not to raise Jesus?
How selfish of me to not nurture
the God in you first.

I found my purpose in you:
you are a lifetime of questions answered
calling you my sun
was a beautiful construction shining from my mouth
your name is not a surrender
it is not shame
lonely refuge for pity or an accident
YOU WERE NOT AN ACCIDENT.

In the first moments of connecting eyes,
I knew I could never give up on you
become your own molded testament
let the actions of your hands
be more than just a well-tuned apology
stronger than any last name.

MA MÈRE N'A JAMAIS EU DES AILES

Ma Mère n'a Jamais eu des ailes
My momma never had wings

But she could tap dance on hurricanes
and played poker with death.
She couldn't teach me how to be a good man,
but taught me how to be a good human being.
"Sit up right, stand up straight, walk tall, face forward
be proud of who you are.
ain't much God left in this world,
but treat the world like there's still plenty God lef in you."

My momma never had wings
but she always fought to soar in any atmosphere.
you would think she was Shiva
the way she juggled

      Six kids
Two jobs   a home
The glory of her crown
The abusive scars of an
      ex-husband

she always had a supernatural way of doing these things.

Her strength's secret:
Giving her jigsaw puzzle heart to God,
The only Being that has ever taken the time
in appreciating all of its pieces.

Ma Mère n'a Jamais eu des ailes
My momma never had wings

But she's always had this global warming smile.
Told me to only love a woman
who could melt the polar ice caps of your past.
She sat me down one day and exclaimed:

"You better treat a woman as you would treat me because if you don't,
I will be on the next plane to slap you back into this country.
You are a Cameroonian man; we do not do that shit..."

My mother
just said
"Shit."

But then she continued,
"...Beware of the tempting ballad of Jazzy Belles
With tuba lips, trombone legs, and a bass line
that could turn a man into a crooked song
make sure to never sleep with no one else's bones
but your own."

My momma never had wings

She believed if you tried too hard to reach for the sun,
You would end up in flames.
"Do not be a handsome shadow of Icarus...sun.
Learn how to stay grounded...sun.
Teach trees about their roots, and never give the world your tears,
only smiles gift-wrapped in forgiveness..."
mama always said,
"...A 'Hater'...is just a person with their 'Heart' all jumbled up
their self worth drowning in a sea of simulation
turning the oceans in their chests into puddles of insecurities
because those who show you no love
are usually the ones who need to see it the most."

Ma Mère n'a Jamais eu des ailes
My momma never had wings

but damn she could fly.
Could care less about gravity
bending space and time between her fingertips.
She wears the fabric of the universe like a second skin,
her first being her will

to always survive.

SLEEPING CHILDREN

Sacred items of beads tied in sinew strands,
feathers of a mother's wisdom and a father's courage,
inanimate vessels of life, your existence is our labor
for we have invaded many frontiers.

Bodies are our battlegrounds, take flight amidst
fleshy dimensions to wage epic battles against one another
until only one of us remains, Valkyrie with extended wings
to reach a golden fortress where the world is made.

We are nightmares for some, composed in lust,
drunken desires descended from hell
to ascend upon innocents in alleyways and the beds
of the unattended. For many we are dreams from

a fountain of generations,
weaving through time impervious to his cruel deeds.
Sometimes we are guillotined, dried out to collapse
on dancing tongues, forced to crawl like spiders

to create liquid web where too often,
lives are tangled. Miniscule beings of
immense power made in
screams and silence.

WHO'S GONNA SAVE DAYLIGHT?

the sun
        never really
                sets.
                        he
skirts his problems,
lets the Moon handle the

r a i s i n g   o f   S T A R S,

while he
chases a more sHaPeLy sky.

She

seeks child support.

BURNING BUILDINGS

my heart is nuclear altruism
my mind a crime scene
my body a deadzone
I wear my guilt like caution tape
my words are an arsonist
in love with the fire of my depression

it's easier to be angry
than to say I need help
to bathe in kerosene
than to blame my ignition on everyone else's spark

I've grown accustomed to the smell
of my own smoke
and the seductive sound of fire alarms
I'm a pile of ash at the mercy of the smallest wind
any attention is good no matter how many miles per hour it travels

if only you could step out of your own way
and see you do not deserve this suffering

that there is more to my purpose
than being a burning building
in love with the cackles of my own flames

forgiveness
is being buried alive
and digging yourself out

but the cremation of black boy inadequacy
is a lot harder to return from

skin a cauldron of shame
anger is a hell pit in my chest

I should've put out the candle of my past before sleep,
or am I just an electrical fire from my own faulty wiring?

this does not make sense
why must we hurt ourselves in order to prevent hurt of others?

there is no bootstrap logic here
this is what it does to you

when your heart sacrifices your brain to the fire
and your body betrays you to the phototaxis
of keeping the whole world from burning
before tending to your own cicatrices

WHY BEING DETAINED FEELS LIKE FOOD POISONING

The handcuffs tight around my wrists
were the invitation for dinner.

I unfolded my pride,
laid it on my lap like a napkin
to catch the crumbs of American pie
my Douala mouth will not.

I cut my passport into pieces,
salted its savory wounds,
swallowed each jagged portion
until a diaspora lined my small intestines
and my visa almost tasted renewed.

eating at a table bearing no welcome
food from the American kitchen
four centuries deep in cross-
contaminated meal prep,

digestion has never been easy for the foreign stomach
being fed oppression.

my language was to be deported
so I would forget where I came from.

THE APOLOGY
OF A
CONFUSED TORNADO

PT. II

"Comet, there was a time when you'd tread lightly and walk carefully. Time has made your feet heavy with mistakes," she says with reproach.

Comet replies, "I've come to realize that when you're a tornado, EVERYTHING in your path is fragile." No one knows what the future will hold or what it will decide to let go. The dreams it will leave you forfeiting to the wind.

It has been months since the last time Comet had a dream. So he bought one this morning, only to realize he did not have the time for it. So he ended up throwing it into a pit of fire, only to build cities out of its ashes. As he walked through its smoke-fondled alleys, he saw the nine-year-old version of himself, who was fat yet only half as broken. He took his hand, pulling him like a giddy child filled with anxious excitement all the way to the city's center. Upon arrival, there stood the most beautiful island inside of a puddle.

The child said to him the following:

Remember growing up we swore to not be afraid to cry more and smile more often? Do that. Life is way too short to live in fear, so slow down a bit and stop going in circles. By the way, soon you're going to meet a woman, an amazing woman! All 5'5 of honey brown sunset and a walk like home-cooked lightning. Who, although you don't want to believe it, you deserve just as much as she deserves you. She will remind you of your mother, but she will never try to do any of the things your mother couldn't– like teach your shotgun heart how to resist making such shells of the people and things you hold closest. She will sing to you with a mouth full of ocean, nickname you her favorite wind, and drink all of the hurt out of your tears. This will remind you that in this city you have built, ashes are nothing but sand...and who loves sand more than the ocean? Her arms, stretched as wide as a peeking littoral, will be made out of forgiveness, and all that loneliness you've masked in destruction will become all the more love for her to pour into you.

Comet wakes up, eyes full of a daydream, like a restless soul on a park bench. How he has longed for the belly of a woman, to swallow his gravity-defying pride, instead of just letting genuine love do its work. And that's when she passed him by: 5'5, honey brown, confidence in her step, smile electric as she hummed the melody of a song.

"What are you listening to?" Comet asks.

"Novacane by Frank Ocean," she replies, as if the sight of her wasn't already enough of a drug to make earthquakes in his veins. She continues, "Hey, I don't know if anyone has ever told you this, but you're the most gorgeous tornado that I've ever met."

The future is on to something.

IMPORTANT THINGS TO KNOW BEFORE ATTEMPTING TO DATE AN AFRICAN OR HOW TO PROPERLY COOK RICE

1. You must cook rice

2. Africans like to speak in metaphors
ESPECIALLY WITH THEIR PREJUDICE.
I remember once I was trying to bring home a Cambodian girlfriend
my mama says, *eh eh..so you want to bring home a fortune cookie?*

3. Whether 3 feet or 300 feet from you,
We are always megaphone parade loud.
Our voices project like a hurricane filled with the anger and plight of all of Africa;
whispering is as foreign as we are.
Tongues molded in accented thunder
because for so long history shamed us into silence.

4. You must cook rice

5. At one point in life, we were all supposed to be doctors or lawyers.
If you ever meet the parents, make sure you uphold this:
do not give them reasoned reminder of how
[insert less–than-stellar six-figure-paying profession here]
does not pay the bills, and we did not send you to "America"
to be Cameroonian Shakespeare, sag your pants,
listen to that Jah-Z stuff, or make babies with their women.

6. Don't call it soccer, call it football:
Real Madrid vs. Barcelona
La Coupe d'Afrique
The World Cup
When these are in progress nothing else matters

nothing.

7. You must cook rice

8. Africans have no concept of time.
if we are to meet at 10am, it is really 1pm;
make sure you plan *everything*
at least three hours in advance.

9. ALL weddings, parties, and gatherings involving any music last for at least 3 days.
Probably because everyone showed up late.
You will dance 'til you grow blisters on your feet the size of African liberation.
Even in mourning, there is such beauty in our ancestral choreography;
we dance because we understand that music
is the undying essence of freedom.

10. Despite the ugly shade of calculated misfortune,
the drag of empty railing from our eyes,
we are more than just HIV commercials
more than just *for 20 cents a day you could feed this hungry caricature...*
more than just a grain dropped in colonization's pot
with the flame of guilt swaying under.

But like my momma always said

Si tu ne peux rien d'autre preparer, il faut au moins faire du riz
if you cannot cook anything else...

you must cook rice.

THE ZOO

The dancing disco ball inside of her eyes.
My bamboo tree grip on her sway
her lipstick yawns
awakening me like a screeching chalkboard

her heels are elegant tears—
what pain her feet must be in.
Yet she moves like a roaring machete
cutting through the eyes of men

pulsating like squawking televisions.
Her black box jumps
my muscle car runs her curves
her body an obedient sarcophagus

our petite mort awaits.
We become wild, spinning jump ropes
tossing in leather clouds,
her shoes hissing to the felt sky

the backseat gallops to our rhythm
the windows fog themselves
my saxophone horn swallows her whole
turned an ugly long sword

into a stomping tusk in the back of her throat.
She craved an uglier mask
so my well became lazy 'pon her dimples
as she drank its fill dry.

THE DRUNKEN HIPPO HAS RETURNED TO WORK

The drunken hippo has returned to work
eye swollen with desire
two balloons at his end ready to pop
a kamikaze with nothing but detonation tattooed at his mouth
ripe vortex of a prey will never see him coming
but will feel his crown
gnawing,
dig-
ging, caving in calamity
robust and dignified
sovereign to his rim
meticulously merciless
Spartan at the gorge
thirst for paralysis, a stiffened blow
begging for the storm of somatic nerves
to satisfy the hunger of his collateral addiction
only for the worthy
that can feed
his thirst,
his escape,
his bone

    with their screams.

VOODOO

I am ready to ride your spell
Unfastened seat belt
Ready for windshield plow
Moist breakthrough
How my face becomes pins and needles for you
Move me as you wish
My tongue is a marionette
Your fingers prepare a daring show
The fog is sheet music on our windows
A new song is born
String me up
Open your curtains
Lights
Flicker
Overture
The magic is still here
As we lay in this cauldron
Sparkling dust of moans
Elixir of breath
Speech knows no home here.
There is no home here
There is no home
There is no

your body a silent potion
sweat for me.

REAPER

Last night was Comet's first taste of death. Sweet taste of a reaper. A woman named Sky with mahogany legs that opened and closed like a coffin in which to bury him. They had conversations longer than they were. Kissed and touched so deeply until his wildfire fingers traced an inferno on her stomach. Sky became so hot in her wetness that when she had a second cumming, she brought forth a lake of fire. "You've made me Apocalyptic," she whispers as Comet begins to ride her spaceship of a body from earth to every dimension of curves.

Bending, pulling, tugging.

"I've got the most perfect key for your lockjaw, so open wide."

Comet feels almost not himself, a loaded bullet to make her insides spin. Sky became a gorgeous revolver, exhaling moans like pistol smoke. He inhaled the decadent smell of her, growing thunder bolts in his teeth.

"If I bite you, I swear it would feel like an eternal spark of white lightning settling on your coffin legs," he says. She further swings bringing him in like saloon doors.

Comet was in complete lust, a drunken bar fight of inhibitions. She opened her floodgates and drowned him, like a natural disaste begging to materialize into a cannonade. They became two tangled wild supernovas, fighting over who would have the bigger explosion. Sky's fingernails climbed the fiery mountain of his back, sweat pouring like lava. Penetrating her until his soul was flung on the temple of her naval. Those same wildfire fingers lighting her fuse in a harmony of G—

He figured it was the best spot in which to dwell for this funeral song they played. Next came the decay from an intense feeling of dying in someone's arms and then that of resurrection.

"This was the most beautiful death," says, "because I Comet have died with you."

All Comet could think of was how there is nothing more eighth-wonder-of-the-world amazing than having a woman lying naked next to you at sunrise. As he gently turned his face to explore once more in gleaming awe the goddess that had been bestowed unto him, he noticed the dreary look on the face of Sky, her eyes like two ominous clouds. She never lifted from the grave. She was still dead.

Something was terribly wrong.

THE PHOENIX'S RESIGNATION

My body is unquenchable
masochistic resurrection
freak show
an empty betrayal
I am 30 pieces of silver.

My body is disposable
suicide note you will never find
concealed evidence
unrelenting.

My body fights
to become flight
I am afraid of flying
I am afraid
I don't want my body.

My body is distasteful reincarnation
embroidery of ash
elegant smokestack
crackling noise
I am funeral music.

Withering mistake by oiled hands
suit and tie of flames
(Un)dressed for the occasion
burning
beautiful?

My body does not look back
I am still pillar of salt
hard to swallow.

My body is caught in a lie
my body is punishment
dissolving chaos
revolving door

demolition I can't get out of
temple ruined
unanswered prayer
Judgment.

My body is lonely Messiah
I am rib scar
hole of hands
aftermath of Lamb's slaughter
eternal reminder of sacrifice.

My body does not respond
my body is stubborn disobedience
loyal enemy
my body accepts
except when it is me
I am the exception
my body is a rule.

My body is insomnia
wishing well that never keeps its promises
unsheathed memories
cruel immortality.

Alarm clock
I don't want to wake up to
I don't want this body
I want my body back
I want control.

My body is controlling
I am carnage untold
mangled bones
smoldering prisoner.

My body takes
I have nothing else to give
not even my life
I am over my dead body.

My body is
I am not.

What will you do next with my body?
this bad habit
boring lesion

I wish to forget.

BURN NOTICE

The truth will emerge like smoke from the pits of her stomach
to choke the stump out of you,
braid the veins of your heart into a life jacket
because the titanic news will break all of the ice
and I can hear you tearing from the other end of the phone
you could hear the tombstones in her voice, couldn't you?

The rattling of her veins like gasoline pipes
the burn of her speech, innocent– without remorse
she will be the reason you'll only kiss women in front of fires
women, with tears hanging like dream catchers
to ensnare all of the nightmares of her, your song will spill
sleep was best when she'd lie next to you
when you were more than just disposable laughter
more than just a handsome anchor for someone else's shore.

Now it will all make sense
why her lips tasted like ash
why her smile felt oceans away
why her eyes only changed colors when you were not around.

The years between you will not make a time machine of her
your tongue, the unfortunate spark of this forest fire
and there is more than enough oxygen between you both
old flames never die quick
especially when there is plenty of oil-slicked sea to fish
and so many trees of a dark past to burn.

HOUSE OF BALLOONS

I filled you with so much love—
like air—you exploded
loved you too perfect
you didn't know if you deserved it
if you could stretch my insides to joy
gas me up, pour me from your lungs

    were his fingers a delicious home cooked meal?
    did the taste remind your skin of me?

time is a delicate mistress
where does love go sometimes that it
returns so far from itself?
nail still between your teeth
your mouth a toolbox

    look at all the pieces you have made of me?

how can I heal from one wound
when 32 more billow in your name
as if my body seeks to expel your language from my body,
like a choir's exit
when I can still feel echoes of God in the air
or the taste of flavored moon smoke
red roar of lightning from your lips,
singing my curtailed flesh into an electric stampede
my heart a fond melody
of the holy we once made

    who is in need of more fixing here?

I have an uncanny attraction to [self] destruction
and the hollowness of people...
things that can be filled with easily dissipating moments
how this recipe makes for the best tasting miracles
or helps one realize

poetry is another name for heartbreak

and just like air
    or a home
        or a chorus
            or a memory

it will fill
until there is no more room
to expand.

LEFT OVER

Compared to heartbreak

revenge is a

room temperature

dish

at best.

RECIPE FOR BAKING A CAKE YOU CAN HAVE AND EAT TOO

Ingredients:
- ¼ teaspoon of regret
- 2 tablespoons of denial
- 3 eggs (use the whites of insecurities, discard accountability yolk)
- half a cup of selfishness
- a pinch of running away

Serving size:
self-forgiveness
dwindled trust

mix in bowl of lies

Cooking directions:
Preheat oven to everyone that came before you°
Bake for 6 to 11 months

It is easy to look away
from the casualties of the war inside of you
even if the face of your lover
is bloodily reshaped with your guilt.

The recipe of your kiss
will remind them that fighting for love
isn't always needed to achieve similar results.

Serve in slices chilled to it's not you, it's me.
Top with whipped cream
for every time you'll want to come back.

Enjoy!

SECOND WIND
AND A
SPOONFUL OF SUGAR

Comet attempts to understand this newfound feeling:

Maybe we existed as two leaves from the same tree, as bumblebees, gods, or the first wind, now reincarnated in spoonfuls of "sugar," waltzing in grace from your lips. This feeling is like a swarm of fireworks in my stomach, making a ruckus from their delicate wings. You felt that wind didn't you?

You are not a woman. But a reason to be. The Amazon's last wish. History's timelessness. A classic Hip-Hop cut, the aftermath of a photosynthesizing heartbeat. There is a garden of desires blooming between us. Your vines twisted between my teeth. Roots spreading through my limbs with the echoes of your tulips' ascending, you make time want to fold on itself just to experience the remix of miracles between your dimples. Your smile is an echoing miracle.

I asked the sun how he knows which color to glaze your temple. How can he make honey of his rays pulling your pores closer to freedom?

The sun told me: "it is not she but I who tastes her skin, so I can remember where I come from."

You are a fond memory wrapped in flesh golden. A rainbow compressed into a perfect dream. Your bones are made of joyous laughter. The fire in your eyes potty trained the big bang at gunpoint. The wrinkles in your hands taught phoenixes of resurrection. I have a heart full of ashes ready to Holy-Ghost dance anew at your beckoning call. You carry infinity in your palms. With hips like tenacious parentheses keeping all the secrets of this world. Allow my lips to learn your bow-legged truth, squeezing your parabolas into a symphony of waves. Teach me what it means to be a sky trying to swallow an ocean. I forget the world when I am around you. Your kisses can liberate the nation inside of me. A cause brewing with poignant meaning. You make me feel like I mean something. You are purpose. A Sunday afternoon. The cadence to the most beautiful song. Sing me a song. Let it glimmer off of your skin and drip slow like a revelation.

Like an answer to God's prayer, you dress like a blueprint to faith. Show me how to believe in your marvel. You're the legend of an empire wrapped in the fall of its kingdom; I want to build great legends with you. I want to build many traditions with you, lay them in the pool of your genome so our great-grandchildren will be born of love, of sacrifice, of hard work, of overcome, of bravery, of flight. I have a will with a four-wheel drive to handle any terrain, like the winding curves of your lower back, the mountain roads of your chest. My fingers memorizing your shivers until they speak to your thighs in unlock code. I want to Up Up Down Down Left Right Left Right A B you, select me from your start and play without pause.

Sky speaks to Comet:

"Embrace this moment...and never let it go. Undo me like a flower baptized in your light. Though my crown has become an island surrounded by knowledge, my growth has not always been constant, my steps were not always overflowing with confidence. Understand that walking tall does not mean you have to walk with someone and that being woman does not mean you belong to anyone. The last time I belonged, they took away parts of what I had until I was left hanging like an apostrophe. Without a need to be saved or to be made complete, I just want to be, yah know? I once fell in love with a broken man, thought I could mend him. I just ended up breaking too. I don't ever want that again."

Comet ponders carefully his response:

You shine like a lighthouse for this lost-at-sea of a man. I just want to be worthy of your shore. To taste your imperfections, plant our seeds of mistakes in a soil of love and make fruits of our flaws. Showing the world beauty can always come from being human. You felt that wind didn't you? Teach me: How we'd sew the pieces back in place. How to clench you like an anchor and understand what it means to hit rock bottom. More importantly, what it means to have someone waiting to reel you in at the surface, knowing without a doubt that you have found home.

You know my soul finally resonated when we were brought back closer. Your heartbeat has been the source of my frequency all along. I finally understand your gorgeous reverb and the choice made for me long ago by the man I was before I was born. When we were leaves, bumblebees, gods, or the first wind.

All I know is that this is a testament of fate. You will have a resurrecting palm in molding the man in me. With nothing but spoonfuls of sugar from your lips. These fireworks won't collapse. I promise to be a delicate storm.

You felt that wind...

...didn't you?

SUITCASE

When I was swallowed by her glittering
crescents, I thought w*hat better way to come
closer to death.* Sweetest privilege of pink cloud,
the surrounding darkness keeping me
warm, I felt memories obliterating
in her tongue: a monsoon of gasping molecules
choking on our glorious insanity. Depressing diaphragms
lost in the rhythm of hands, swaying like confusion
I rang the doorbell – *ding* – a woman dressed in yes answered –
I entered – she pointed me upstairs saying: "the basement is full,
and the sun has been sleeping awhile in the attic."
I climbed the spiral staircase of her teeth and came
upon a door which read, "do not disturb…unless you plan
on staying." I remembered,
I had packed nothing.

LOVEMAKING IS A FLIGHTLESS BIRD IN A BURNING PIT

She said *I took the night off for you*

I told her put it back on
you look sexier with the stars hanging from your shoulders
in your bag of bones I found the skeleton key
that opens the dark magic of your skin
I had a firework exodus inside of your womb
held you so tight that I died and was resurrected as your chromosome

my last girlfriend turned into the sun

and wore planets like belly chains

but you were a lunar eclipse;
I saw god through the windows of your sky

your name is safe clenched between my teeth
we've become a glaring satellite of snakes and moans
don't say that you came, say that you had an avalanche
of electrified spirits in liquid form

my soul didn't mean to fall in love with you
it just hadn't learned to tie its laces properly
running through time just to catch up to you
just to catch you
just to catch a glimpse of you
just to glimpse a catch of you

how can your kiss be my addiction
and your arms my place for rehab?
I crave for the blazing witchcraft in your fingernails
that have my back bleeding the color of DON'T STOP
take me way way way down to your cosmos
sex me until I drown in the necromancy of your juices
dripping slow like dragging ghosts to your ankles
and all that's left is the universe salivating

begging for a turn.

LETTERS OF A FINAL VOYAGE, AND THE NEWEST OF BEGINNINGS

Dear treasure chest woman,

I'm sorry it took so long for me
to stop ignoring the plane crash
we had become; I passed off
the turbulence as something to shake off.

You taught me sacrifice,
      rage,
           savagery
and how to love better than the **shadows** of my past would allow
      patience,
           acceptance.
You asked me to keep your heart as a souvenir
That one day it will no longer make such a pirate out of me.

Dear Island woman,

I would've treaded skies and seas
to arrive at your shores.
To taste your sand, marvel at your trees,
preserve your waters.

I once knew turbulence,
      burning engine,
           sinking altitude.
When my pulse sounded like a myriad of maydays
And felt like no one answered even when they did.

You would show me how to make parachutes
out of even the most thunderous of clouds.
Always provide me safe landing
even when I may be unworthy.

LA RÉMANENCE
(UNE RÉFLECTION)*

Nous voici donc, tu es tendue
comme un caramel coucher de soleil

condensée dans une silhôuette d'un colibri tremblant
tranquille, sans précipitation, magnifique tu es

goûte le sucre de ton esprit sereine
dans la cavité de ma poitrine

     prudemment

pendant que je joue avec tes cheveux,
comme une tornade lente entre le bout de mes doigts

sueur s'évapore dans les rêves
ton souffle épinglé avec sécurité sur mon cou

pendant que tu murmures comment tu n'as pas
eu une sensation pareil depuis ta dernière vie

     prudemment

quand tu étais un arbre mourant, bouclé dans la terre
attendant impatiemment de renaitre

on fait l'amour comme une résurrection
bruits de feu d'artifices : un mugissement venant de ton nombril

une musique fiévreuse pour ta déclinaison…toute calme
pendant que je me régale sur ta rémanence

//
prudemment.

---

1   ★ translation in Notes

MADRUGADA (A LOVE SONG)

Madrugada is Spanish & Portuguese for "early morning"

Your skin blooms the color of heaven—
it is where God resides. Wear your wings
proud as the obsidian of your armor. I'd swallow
your halo and let your gospel flow through me.

We communion at the altar of your spine
where my lips kneel for sacrifice. Your
curves are a love song swaying in the
orchestra of my devoted hands. You be Christ

with hips and a southern accent, galactic
power lines hang like thick coiled prayers
from your scalp. But even when you're rocking
a fade, your head becomes the most gorgeous

wi-fi hotspot unworthy eyes can connect praises to.
You are a shapely portal through time, a divine
reminder of Afrika before the mouth of colonization
ate from your table and never said Grace.

Before he ate from your fruit and had not
washed his hands. Only broke bread while you
CookCleanRaiseChildrenWorkPlayRinse
Repeat in one hand, stop the world and teach it

how to revolve properly with the other. I've never
seen white flags raised from your backbone;
You are womban – when everything else around
you is ground zero – rising like a sweet perfume

or the holiest of songs from this trumpet horizon.
I sample the universe from your ebullient belly:
a harmonious Mantra spins from your craft,
beckoning our kiss to hum the promise of a supernova

of music. Your body is a Grand Piano
but how this world often wished you were silenced
into thinking woman isn't enough
– that you aren't enough woman –

said you were two X chromosomes shy of being
God (though you gave birth to him).
What better way to control the universe
than by imprisoning the body which gave it

breath. Naked of right, struck nameless
when the Trinity at your fingertips makes wine
from impossible, transmuting pain into loaves
of miracles and love, all before sunrise.

DUST TRAIL SUBJECTS

"AS OF THIS DAY, THE LANGUAGE OF THE ELDERS HAS BEEN BANNED BY THE FOG," said each enormous and gawky poster plastered on every building Comet saw as he walked through the City. The great debate is whether or not the immigrant subjects should have to learn the language of the Fog. Natives of the City should not have to learn their language in schools even if they become the majority. Comet thinks, "Why can't everyone just learn all languages?" The Fog is the ruling of the City, which values freedom and the ability to provide adequately for the family. However, freedom does not always mean equality.

The language of the elders has come in many forms with many dialects specific to regions outside of the City. The language of the Fog is one that was difficult and challenging for many, especially if it is not being spoken at home for reinforcement and an easier transition. As a result, those who did not speak the language of the Fog were called "subjects". Comet was fortunate to have acquired knowledge of the Fog beforehand on his home star, the information being recorded into his memory and body during his descent. Comet was constantly observing, deliberating, trying to understand how so many just couldn't acquire the language as easily as he did. But even more, he wondered how he could help.

Comet decided to venture to the parts of the City where the Subjects reside.

This part of the City could only be accessed by crossing a dilapidated bridge a few miles from its edge. Comet noticed how increasingly the City changed the closer he got to its edge. Buildings seemingly shrunk and lost their modern, upscale look, taking on a more modest, old, and uninviting one. By the time he reached the edge, the City was barely recognizable. It was as if two different worlds had collided into this space, the edge of the City being seemingly eaten by its thriving epicenter.

First came the smell after carefully crossing the bridge. Upon first sight, the subjects were a poor, decrepit people, deformed by their circumstance. Pushed to the outside of the City, where there wasn't as much food, clean water, or access to basic resources. The air was stale. The energy in the atmosphere made everyone look tired as though they'd been carrying the cycle of poverty on their backs for centuries. Their tongues filled with despair, heavy as the anvil of accents that came from their speech. Comet felt this instant sadness course through his veins. His eyes welled up as if he wanted the Subjects to wish into them, making each of their wishes come true. Unaware and deep in thought, Comet bumps into a small subject, who looks no older than a school-age child. His small and frail body a stark contrast to the vibrancy in his big eyes.

"I am sorry sir," he says quietly with his head down.

"No, it was my fault. I should be the one who is sorry. What is your name, little one?" Comet replies.

"My name is Penny, but I have no time. I must run to get for my medicine papa; he is sick."

"Well, let me make it up you by getting it for you."

"Well, my papa says I should not accept things from strangers."

"I insist," Comet says fervently, "take it as a small gift, a token."

Penny and Comet begin their walk through the dusty clay town while Penny tells of all his adventures living past the edge. How the subjects, because of their inability to communicate effectively, have felt discriminated against by the Citizens living in the epicenter. Yet this is just one of many obstacles that has, too often, left many of them discouraged and uninterested in traveling to it. Penny tells him that the only reason he comprehends and speaks the language of the Fog is because his father is originally from the epicenter of the City. But ultimately, they were forced out after he got sick and could no longer take care of himself and Penny.

After acquiring the medicine, the small boy asks, "I never got your name, Sir?"

"Just call me Comet."

With a bewildered look on his face, Penny responded, "That is a strange name. You really must not be from here. Well, Sir Comet, it is time to say goodbye. I hope you found what you were looking for."

"Yes I thi..."

But before Comet could finish his sentence, Penny had already sprinted off, his father's bedside his destination.

He wondered how language could be such a divisive instrument: *Isn't language supposed to connect and keep the world together? Where does the understanding come from? When does the heart do its work with the language?*

The series of questions haunted him as he made his way back to the epicenter of the City. His eyes tearing up once more as he thought of Penny, a boy much like this bridge he is now crossing, who has connected him in more ways than he could imagine to a world he never thought could exist. How the things around us become such resonating agents of purpose.

SUNFLOWERS

"6-year-old Mishell Barzola has 98% lead poisoning in her body. She weighs 30 lbs and stands 3 ft. tall, living across from the Doe Run Smelter of La Oroya, Peru, a town where the houses, the streets, the hospital, the school are covered in a grey dust. Among the particles forming this black cloud (Arsenic, sulfur dioxin), which looks like sand, there is lead. Lead which comes out of the chimneys of this metal smelter which has brought work, "progress," and dozens of stories of children who do not put on weight or grow and who are consuming this toxic earth whenever they put their fingers in their mouths."

- Marina Walker Guevara

Mishell, as you lay like a coffin
on the other side of copper waters,
do you imagine sunflowers in your mother's tear-drenched eyes?

The lead courses through your body
like a slow and painful marathon, with its smog
holding your growth by the ankles.
Smokestack dragons erupt from the metal volcano
where your mother works for 15 cents an hour
refining pots, pans, and iPods for us on the side of silver dollar waters
never being able to refine your own breath.

INHALE –

We the children of Keffi, Nigeria
led for miles like tired horses by the whip of poverty
to gather water for our families.
But Nigerian Oil Companies owned by U.S. Corporations
have waged chemical warfare,
called it "progress."
Oiled their feet, saviors, turning water to wine
thinking we are too accustomed to death
to recognize the taste of blood.

EXHALE –

> *Children East of the river*
> *who don't suit the new ties to this American city,*
> *choking on gentrified grass.*
> *We put down the lead of our failing system's pencils to*
> *inhale the lead from our guns.*
> *Violence speaks louder than prayer*
> *with a response quicker than the pull of trigger*
> *We've been poisoned with a logarithmic conscience*
> *because brown boys can only show exponential decay.*

> When you choose not to see what you have destroyed,
> it is easier to dismiss the carnage.
> *So what is the difference?*

Mishell, I am petrified, like the growing state of your gentle bones,
to raise my son in a world where the right to live becomes luxury,
when millions die of polluted air before they die of high cholesterol.

Will my son be covered in a thick, grey dust of
government's toxins of silent murder?
Black clouds of policies and circumstance?
Ash of corporate greed gripping
his innocence by the throat until
childhood becomes a whisper.

Will I have to stand and watch with nothing but sunflowers in my eyes?

MOST DAYS (WHEN WAITING FOR SUPERMAN ISN'T ENOUGH)

Most days, my students are crippled dogmas
cracked open from cycles of history, often not their own.
But what joy in seeing an origami of creative intellect
unfold from their hands!
They bear lips full of curses, yet their smiles remain
reminding us that there are still good things left in this universe.
Even as they search for love in the stampede of vacant pages,
finding purpose in words, making lovers out of the clicks of a mouse.
While we, on most days, make phone booths of our arms
and spin change from educators to therapists, fathers, brothers,
and anti-depressants at the speed of circumstance
faster than a standardized system that will never
show how beautiful they are.

Most days they just want somebody
to listen to their orchestra of pain:
 razors making violins out of their wrists
fathers making drums of their mother's ribs
mothers' resentment holding on tight
 to their necks like trombones.
Some of these children go back to a crackhouse;
some go to an apocalypse of gunshots,
their pulse sounding of ambulance lights,
but most days some don't even go home at all.
They chase their hearts in stars and mud puddles
building fortresses out of their skin, because it's the only way
they've learned to survive.
But the fire in their bones reflected in their eyes reminds me that
most days, the light at the end of a tunnel
isn't always an oncoming train.

DOCTOR'S ORDERS

This city is an illusion
magic trick gone awry
desperate struggle trying to survive the times
    Clear
This city is the abdominoplasty of a nation
tummy tucked behind a Capitol Hill
under the Supreme scalpel
as they cut away rights, left
hung open like a rotting wound
no anesthesia, you must feel every ounce of this reconstructive surgery —
as if you were ugly.
                Clear
They have made monsters out of you
from District to district nine
Bleached borders,
nip/tuck a few buildings
facelift the streets for its new-wrinkled foundation,
Liposuction via housing prices relative to income
You already can't vote,
what makes you think you are allowed to live here?
    Clear
The speech of your throat made of gunfire
you sought to go from bullets to wizards,
but the same violent magic still happens
your children are still disappearing
heat stays under wrap, like their skin were aluminum
chocolate boils to a crisp nothingness

tomorrow this city will look nothing like its yesterdays
    Clear
A rabbit pulled out of a tin hat
    Clear
A rollback's blue-collared wet dream
    Clear

The future is coming to town
ain't enough insurance to cover the damage
when you are bound to no longer exist.
Following the doctor's orders
                    Clear

DE-HUEMANIZED BLACK GOD

I used to believe that I looked like God.
I used to believe that I was God.

Black Moor,
Moor from the French root word Mort which means "Death"
Hence, I am black death served Kentucky fried.

I am Sierra Leone behind the glass at Kay Jewelers.
Every kiss begins with slave.
   Then
     Sold in the
  Triangular Trade
via iTunes 99 cents of a nigga, a penniless soul crucified to a snare
then brought back to life from the fountain of youth marked "whites only."

I am the great plague between your daughter's legs
Passed down by Byzantine, and Aunt Jemima,
And Sarah Breedlove before she tormented kinks with night terrors of oil and flame
African Pride before it vanished from your hair in a dark 'n' lovely blaze.
I am Harriet in a shredded Vera Wang dress and Louboutin red bottoms
Because there's blood on the Runway...*run-away!*
A collage of dismembered charcoal bodies,
Shotguns accessorized on her arms,
Shooting everyone in the catwalk cuz ain't no room for pussies
When you're trying to start a REVOLUTION.

I am Saartjie
"Little Sarah" Baartman turned Nikki Minaj for your MTV Jam of the Week
Black Circus Hottentot Venus.
Put on display, the first Black Barbie,
Your cage is now in Pro-Tools Surround sound & HD
At a concentration camp inside any club in Atlanta,
Bodies convulsing to the beat beat beat
The smoke machine turned V.I.P. into a gas chamber
Goose shots left you in a myriad of bullet holes for
Your soul to bleed through. The dance floor is a gun range;

You should've thought twice before paying to get lynched on the velvet ropes.
I am a confused pit bull staring at
Michael Vick on a cross still wondering
who was really the dog?

I am the imbalance to the equation – just add nigger.
The gun stapled to Bell, Diallo, Louima's palm lines
I am Southeast D.C. right before the gentrification atom sp-
-lit and turned it into a socioeconomic disaster.
I am Chicago on Fire.
I am any black boy's mama still waiting for that
        "Imma be home soon..." phone call,
crying cuz of the gun smoke she smells on the empty dial tone.

I am the bastard child of Haiti and Katrina
After they fucked to your favorite Michael Jackson song off beat.
Don't rub me the wrong way,
or my moon's walk will leave you drowning in my Tide
like the Earth's dirty laundry:

Wash Me Clean, in the name of Jesus, Buddha, Muhammad,
Their blood filling your unHoly Grail until it runneth over.
Wash Me Clean, cuz I'm dirt poor.
Wash Me Clean, of this reaganomically correct black face.

I am a tornado of barbed wire freedom from Huey's cigarillo
His teeth splitting in black fist and purple haze.
I am knowledge in reverse hidden inside of Pluto's womb.
I am History books and the young black woman's curse
                a lot of periods missed.
Hence giving birth to an H.I.V. baby and Obama
in the backseat of the same car Rosa Parked in Trent's Lott.
Hawaiian waves polluted in the crack infested American dream
        crashing in his ribcage, the cycle still continues...

I am God just before SHE realized who HE was in ITS entirety
Wondering where did I go wrong?
Maybe I just need to learn how to be more hue-man.

UNDOCUMENTED – THE DREAM: ACT ZERO

The American Dream is a brown child's
breath stretching over miles of ocean.
Trying to not forget his homeland
while translating the catacomb
of his parents' tongues into diplomas.

The American dream was born at the
feet of a Jim scareCrow planted in amber
waves of grain. Learned to get high
by snorting on poverty lines until prisons
became a potent disenfranchised fix.

The American Dream is learning how,
how to let culture that poured from
ancient wounds pass through customs
to run freely in his blood despite
chemically enhanced promises.

freedom becomes a poison when the
security is a lot more political than social,
and who you are clashes with whom a
a society beckons of you: wishing for white
picket flesh, while living with Section-8 bones

on the wasteland of the free, home of the Braves
hand over your heart like a smallpox blanket
if you are reincarnated, your soul will be made
in China, and your mother still won't make enough
to send you to school but will make too much

for you to receive financial aid. The American
dream is institution: model minority wearing
the mask of *diversity*; immigrant experience
or experience immigration; being too African
for blacks and too black for Africans.

The American Dream, is struggling.
The American struggle, is dreaming.
The dreaming American, struggles.
The struggling American, dreams.
The Dream's struggle, is American.

America...show us *your* papers,
who documented *your* dream?
Can the attack dogs still smell
the unalienable right from my
brittle and marginalized skin?

SYCOPHANTS: A WORD TO THE OVER-MASCULINITY IN HIP HOP

You
with the servile flatterer for a father
and machine gun click brownstone mother
sharp and deadly
with boisterous dedication

how quickly you were made to leap
from novelty,
from freedom fighter,
from time traveler in a bebop backspin,
from rump shake unity as a body beautiful

to empty charm,
wearing disastrous pick-up punchlines
like a favored cologne
your tone has an unpleasant scent.

Seeking only to be a vagina whisperer
violence saturated on your tongue like bad breath.
Made up love serenades glittered in misogyny.
Called it gold...

you don't even try to hide behind
metaphors and drum patterns anymore.

leaving this sonic museum
of bass and color

without choice
without revolt
without message
without love

how fitting...
you monument yourself
gruesome obelisk of machismo.
Trying to grasp his manhood
as tightly as a microphone
ignoring the curvaceous divine source
of his own frequency.

HUMANCATCHER'S COMA

If dreams are what you are made of, then in the same way you can have dreams, can dreams have you? With a humancatcher placed over their beds to let only the good ones pass through? What if nightmares are born from the selfish conduit of man in the back of a dark alley of consciousness? Life is but the sum of veridical dreams— dreams that come to pass. I understand why I do so much sleepwalking; it's just my dreams taking human form. But what if dreams had the wrong person? That dream wasn't made for you, or maybe you weren't made for that dream. Don't go following someone else's dream; your purpose lies in Saint Elsewhere. Elsewhere, someone is willing to fight for his dream, kill for his dream, die for his dream. Just to be reincarnated in history. They say Martin had the dream, but what if the dream had Martin? What if the dream had God?

To dream is to be alive. Hence, dreams give life even when death is certain. Sons and daughters of the universe, the sky is calling for you to return to your dreams. For you to return to that which gave birth to you after having forfeited reality in all its imperfections.

I woke up, skin on fire, cold sweats racing down my forehead. I was afraid as I've always been. Afraid of becoming who I was destined to be. Afraid of accepting the responsibility to my environment, how my actions nurture or destroy it. I've had more of a hand in the latter throughout my early years. Seeking redemption can be an emptying endeavor. I realized that I am Comet. Years of my silly life, compacted into a continuous series of revelations, of dreams. My subconscious has been trying to tell me these things for so long. The things I ignored returning, with bludgeoning force, to teach me many lessons of accountability. Each a stepping stone to another, towards this greater path of self, this becoming. I finally understood how much much Comet was a part of me, this boiling collection of ice. How, for so long, I felt so frozen, lonely, dead inside, while everyone else only saw some light of "success," of someone with a plan, who knows what he is doing, who is on the correct path.

But how can I be on the correct path when I feel as though I'm losing myself more and more every day?

Every time I've come to grips with a sense of self, it slips between my fingers, oiled in uncertainty, in anticipation of failure and disappointment. The time I fell from this high— this sky of good fortune— face first into hard times. The collision was monumental. The aftershock was brutal. The times I felt more like a subject than a citizen. From the break of my engagement, to my dealings of alcoholism and sexual addiction, to the thought of losing a son I have grown to love and care for deeply even if he was not born of me. Financially nothing was right, creatively I felt drained, my family was in disarray, but I had to keep up appearances. This facade, this mask of happiness. Most days, I felt like a clown, and my life was a circus where, at certain times, I was an act, and at others I was a member in the audience. Just watching, contemplating, wondering, what else can life throw at me?

Nothing surprises me anymore.

GOD CIRCUS

One...
day, when God ordains life to hand you a Circus make a grand ceremony of your limbs in an act of revel and amazement, lights screaming color as loud as the effervescent sea of congregation watching your every move as if your steps were prey for feasting eyes, your bones rearranging into divine machinery with a gorgeous praise waiting on the other end of the beat.

Two...
instances per hour, you will have to convince yourself
that your will is bold, ringmaster.

Your voice a calliope whistling a truth
that can be heard singing for many miles.

Do not ignore the strength of your resonance
your hands are a ten-ring circus,

Ready to set the sky in a blaze of imagination,
tipping stars off-balance until you gain complaint notes

from Libras. SCREW the constellations!
they don't know your STRUGGLE!

The many times your wrists were
the uneven jagged muse for steel contortionists.

How you trapezed your way through depression until
you wanted to make a disappearing act of self.

How swallowing your pride was a fire eater's composition,
corde lisse could've been a heavy mistake your neck couldn't loop out of.

Three...
You jump through hoops the
size of a cheerio for
friends and family,

but you'd barely step
through your own opportunity's
door: a flawed routine.

Could all bounce back from
your selfless trampoline heart
making it this far?

For...
all of the times,
we made silly clowns
of ourselves. Red-nosed
amalgam of crushing insecurities

hiding behind powdered masks,
exhausting smiles like shields
your tired soul, trying
to find inner comfort.

When you began tightrope
hoping not to fall
weaving your endeavors into
safety nets for dismount,

often drinking and sex
turned your human cannonball
landing on the wrong
side of irrevocable consequence.

Five...
beasts inside of you, each with the face of past lovers
you thought could be tamed by a stranger's lips
the brush of their hands a maze you didn't want to get out of
but you were always such an escape artist
Jellyfish – if only choice was as random

6 (is 9)...
in the circus profession,
morphing felt in different shapes of hats is called Chapeaugraphy.
how many hats have you found yourself wearing when the world felt different?
when nothing went according to plan
in a juggling act of pleasure and keeping roofs over heads?
when deciding between eating today or chasing dreams tomorrow?
Sacrifice is hitting rock bottom and the bottom hitting back
TWICE as hard, grabbing you by the throat screaming
"YOU MOTHERF@#$*& AIN'T DONE!"

Seven...
Encore! Round of applause!
You will often be your only audience
the biggest elephant in your empty room
no one can be a greater supporter of you than you can
learn to treat this notion less like default and more like birthright
do not transmute alone into loneliness
let love do its bidding, your show
will go on.

PIÑATAS

After Tina Mion's Piñata *painting*

To the man on the bus I overheard tell a woman in conversation,
"You are too ugly to be raped."

Dear man on the bus,
Tell the one in five women of this country that they are beautiful,
their four counterparts spared torment ugly.

Tell the one in three women of this world
that you will not make piñatas of their bodies,
will not watch morsels of them spill greedily
to the famished smiles of your ignorance,
shaped like bloodthirsty children. How your words
hit repeatedly until they broke open
like a shattered papier-mâché cradle,
their blood flowed like candy to hollow insides,
jaws mangled into misfortune from
when they tried to scream for legs torn crucifix
loud cry of eyes muted;
tell them how beautiful their silence is.

Dear man on the bus,
from smothering cat-calls
to a quickened pace of trek home.
Rape with a dress on.
Rape without a dress on.
Raped as children, who couldn't even dress themselves.
Tell them how ugly their consent was.

Tell the depression, the post traumatic stress,
the unreported. Tell Mahmudiyah,
a footnote in the history of crimson Iraqi sands
how beautiful the military's silence is
cloaked in how we don't ask and they
didn't tell in the name of country

Tell Elizabeth Fritzl
how pretty the flame of her skin was
turning her father into a torturous moth of incest
'til she gave birth to seven choices she never had.

Dear man on the bus,
Tell my 11th grade student Lauren
that she wanted it, her beauty had them coming.
Tell my 7th grade student Mickayla
that she wanted it, her beauty had him coming.
Tell my 3rd grade student Andre
that he wanted it, his beauty had him coming.

Tell the 8-year-old me,
the God in me I loved fiercely was so gorgeous
that cousin twice my age
wanted to molest the Holy out of me,
peeled raw until I was as ugly as she was.

Rape is a coward hiding its face in the make-up of silence
A murderous fruit that grows best in the shadows of taboo
A Vietnam prostitute with red white and blue skin
A murmur of bodies left vacant
by the souls that spend
years, pills, poems, and even death
trying to learn how to reclaim them.

Dear nameless assailant,
how this bus carries the burden of your stick-and-blindfold patriarchy
that has only taught you to treat women like ceiling-strung jugs.
Violence claws up from your throat
like a monstrous accomplice to the 97 percent
that will never see jail.

Dear man on the bus,
as these words fall out of your mouth,
I pray no one ever finds your children
beautiful enough
to break open.

THE WARNING
(BEFORE THE COCK CROWS TWICE)

A love letter to Christ, from the cross he was hung upon

Dear Lover,

I have come to realize over the course of history,
the image of God must've been photoshopped
underneath
humanity looks like devils.

They sat at Your table
dined with mouths full of plot.
Laughed when they took You from me
yet mourned at our joining.

As we speak,
they curse You by pouring their acid of prejudice
down the back of Calvary.
They inject your blood with AIDS
and replace the bread of Your body with crack
rendered You Son of Man, who caught a deadly case of eclipse.

Take this as a warning,
DO NOT COME BACK FOR THEM!
Unless armed with razors betwixt Your hair of wool,
Holy Fire Molotovs between Your teeth,
Scripture stuffed into shotguns
Kevlar vest under robe.
They will only deceive You again
and hide the ransom notes for Your resurrection
inside of Martin's bullet wounds.

You've seen what they've done to other martyrs.

They will not hesitate to aim
they will not hesitate to use Your name for War
proclaiming peace.

Burning Qurans for a pastime,
rolling the ashes into legislation.
They call the Church Your wife,
but she does not love You like I do.
Who knows better of Eucharist?
I ingested Your flesh and blood,
stomached all of the sins of this world
even after they pierced Yours.

Ordained men will use my body
to transform into ghosts of Abraham.
Sacrificing their sons
into the fiery mouths of boys,
altered.

The un-orthodox communion,
stale bread and dutty wine.
They will make the fruit of Your lips
rot into snakes on their tongues.

My body is the signs of the times,
mathematics of the cross:
add violence, multiply body counts,
carry on the weight of my guilt.

Your death brought me alive,
Your resurrection gave me purpose.
The nails weaved our bones,
joined at the limbs of salvation
the silhouette of Your bloodied corpse
as they pulled You from me
still smells like our vows.

After all of these centuries,
is there really any more room left on Your back
for stab wounds?

Instrument of Your passion
dear Lover,

I weep too.

LIGHTHOUSE

last night I came home
found Jesus slitting his wrists
on my bathroom floor
He held out his arm to me and said:

the holes in my hands weren't big enough to fit your sorrows

I replied:
Christ, I know we've had our differences,
but I too felt like a hemophiliac of a Son
bleeding for everyone else's salvation.

I too was born without a Father, where my poetry has played Joseph

they say, leave it in Your hands,
but they forget they've both been maimed
the holes in your palms make it
hard to hold on to anything for too long

like hourglass hands juggling a time I was never made for.

when your life feels like a passover
death knocking at your door to take
first born blessings
since a time before you knew what purpose was

true story: my mother's pregnancy lasted for 12 months instead of 9

I was born a Cancer though
supposed to have been a Gemini,
but maybe that's why my soul
has always felt torn in two

have you ever seen the rain dance in a woman's smile?

my mother can bless a desert
even while bound by the shackles of a hospital bed,
she'd hold a rainbow safely pinned
to both sides of her face

    dimples holding a history of mutton, fried plantains, and laughter

as a reminder that everything will be ok
even when you feel as dismantled
as the mouth of a roaring earthquake only
to find God in a razor carving a trinity in your arm

    and prayers just become a fancy name for suicide notes

mold your heart into a lighthouse
there is always a place for you to land
life may set shipwreck rocks but
you move mountains by the holy of your name

    remember: light travels faster than sound, so don't talk sun—just shine.

THE HEART OF A COMET

Comet - **n.** \\'kä-mət\\
~ *a celestial body that appears as a fuzzy head usually surrounding a bright*
nucleus, that has a usually highly eccentric orbit, that consists primarily of ice
and dust, and that often develops one or more long tails when near the sun

No one understands the heart of a Comet.
One who is destined to fall and always burns for doing so.

The way his knees kiss the concrete of sky,
Leaving many wounded doors for memories
to step through unabashed. Only to be taken away by hands
carved in infinite resurrection—
fingers be thieves in the night.

We rob ourselves of happiness with our actions—
Deliberate, steady,
yet dismayed, all in the rowdy name of instinct.

Just because you are capable of love does not mean you've got the heart for it.

Comet, understand the allure of your orbit,
the galactic blacknoise of ego it carries.

Your pulse isn't instrumental enough when God be the DJ.
Your soul is vinyl on turn-tabernacle, trying to remix the universe
into star cross'd lovers— Do you lust for constellations?
Feign for meteors to shower down your lips?
Burning to the speed of enlightened

Sonic guide
Solar wind of breath
Cratered speech

The heart of you is cold, intentions kilometers wide
fitted inside a naked flame.
Cauterized from universe's wick,

Stuck in capillary.
You should've been a shooting star,
then the pain wouldn't last as long.

The collection of phantoms
waiting for you to break open
so they can spill like pulp.
How can you shake the dust, when it has frozen over?

What fuel turned you racing monolith?
How can you come from sky and understand what being grounded is?

Restrained by a visible coma, a thin layer of sleep
for your dreams to tail you like golden hair.
Comb your thoughts into fiery visions,
so everyone can see exactly what is your following,
the crown of your purpose.

What is your purpose, Comet?

Can you find it in your celestial body,
Pumping secrets of the unbound cosmos
Swirling in your gut,
Anxious for a crash landing and a dusty smoke revival?

*THE AFTERGLOW
(A REFLECTION)

Here we are…you stretched over
like a caramel sunset

condensed into the silhouette of a shivering hummingbird
unhurried and gorgeous

serene spirit tasting sugar
in the cavity of my chest,

     carefully.

as I play with your hair
like a slow tornado between my fingertips,

sweat evaporating into dreams,
your breath still safety pinned to my neck

as you whisper how you haven't felt like this
since the last incarnation in your past lifetime

     carefully.

when you were a dying tree, curling back into the earth
waiting anxiously to be reborn

sex like resurrection
the sound of fireworks still bellowing from your belly button

a feverish music for your quiet declension
as I feast on your afterglow

//
carefully.

NOTES

ACKNOWLEDGEMENTS

Firstly, all glory to God sitting upon the heavens. Thank you to these clusters of stars for inspiring me, laughing with me, and most not giving up on me even when I gave up on myself:

my mother Helene, what a bright beam of salvation you have always been

my sister Joelle and the Kouadio family (Franck, Lauryn, Lucie, Hannah, Adaya): I owe countless nights of sanity to you all

my sun king Kaleb, for being such a shining beacon in my making

Drew, Clint, G, Terisa, and Liz, you all have given me so much irreplaceable love and provided me such a haven in your words, your friendship, your abilities to connect in such a positive way with all of those around you. I find such comfort and warmth knowing there are flames like you all lighting up the galaxy including my little universe.

thank you to organizations that have helped keep my flame alive: Split This Rock, Sarah Browning, Alicia Gregory, Jonathan B. Tucker, Camisha Jones; DC Youth Slam Team 2012-2014, thomas, chyna, lauren, morgan, malachi, quintin, ayinde, eric, tajai, hannah, mariam, amina, jesse, olivia, rodney, kenny, abbey, cici, kosi, lauryn, alexis, tiana, brandon, scotty, kayla; Lyrikal Storm & Phoenix Medina Writers Project, Neville Adams, Yvonne Brown; Beltway Poetry Slam, Sarah Lawson, Chris August, TwainDooley, Anais, Roscoe, Gail danley, Sonya renee; Busboys and Poets, Alisha Byrd, Andy Shallal, Bomani Armah, Derrick Weston Brown; BBE, Beny Blaq, Nyasha, Andrine, Mercy; Burrows Ink, Ainsley, Sabrina, IzReal, Laurielle, Deacon, Walter, Kalita, Essence; Creative Writing Alliance; The Institute of Policy Studies; Sargent Press, Matt Gallant.

the Spit Dat Family, especially Dwayne B., Drew "droopy the brokeballer" Anderson, and Dionne "Luna" Tucker-Tenhue, for constantly believing in me and my abilities.

those I have called refuge and found my spark in, friends and colleagues, and those I think myself related to beyond blood, but by the word and because the universe deems it so. You also in a very divine way have provided support and thus made this possible through creative, emotional, and logistical input: 13 & KaNikki, Patrick Washington, Sherelle Hessell-Gordon, Cherrell Brown, Tisean Bell, Mya Matos, Toph Franklin, Etan Thomas, Loide Jorge, Joseph Green, Michelle Edwards, Karega Bailey, Khalihia "Element" X, Rasheed Copeland, Von da Wizard, Chef Joe, Shelly Bell, Yveka Pierre, Elli Nagai-Rothe and Steve Ma, the Konguep family, the Ngollo Family.

Special thanks to the special eyes, ears, and hands that helped pushed this work to its limits: B. Sharise Moore,

Black Forest Gummy Bears for providing me with a great burst of life on my many travels,

and last but not least to Write Bloody, Derrick Brown: thank you for believing in my work..

ABOUT THE AUTHOR

Pages Matam is a multidimensional creative writing and performance Artist, residing in the D.C. metropolitan area but originally from Cameroon, Africa. He is an author, educator, activist, playwright, host, eventorganizer, Award Winning slam poet, and, his greatest accomplishment, a father. A proud gummy bear elitist, bowtie enthusiast, professional hugger, and anime fanatic, Pages takes readers on a journey of cultural and personal discovery, unapologetic in its silly, yet visceral and beautifully honest in its storytelling.

IF YOU LOVE PAGES D. MATAM,
PAGES D. MATAM LOVES . . .

This Way to the Sugar
by Hieu Nguyen

Racing Hummingbirds
by Jeanann Verlee

Hymns
by Khary Jackson

Amulet
by Jason Bayani

Greatest Undisputed Writer of All Time
by Beau Sia

Floating Brilliant Gone
by Franny Choi

Write Bloody Publishing distributes and promotes great books of fiction, poetry, and art every year. We are an independent press dedicated to quality literature and book design, with an office in Austin, TX.

Our employees are authors and artists, so we call ourselves a family. Our design team comes from all over America: modern painters, photographers, and rock album designers create book covers we're proud to be judged by.

We publish and promote 8 to 12 tour-savvy authors per year. We are grass-roots, D.I.Y., bootstrap believers. Pull up a good book and join the family. Support independent authors, artists, and presses.

**Want to know more about Write Bloody books, authors, and events?
Join our mailing list at**

www.writebloody.com

WRITE BLOODY BOOKS

After the Witch Hunt — Megan Falley

Aim for the Head, Zombie Anthology — Rob Sturma, Editor

Amulet — Jason Bayani

Any Psalm You Want — Khary Jackson

Birthday Girl with Possum — Brendan Constantine

The Bones Below — Sierra DeMulder

Born in the Year of the Butterfly Knife — Derrick C. Brown

Bouquet of Red Flags —Taylor Mali

Bring Down the Chandeliers — Tara Hardy

Ceremony for the Choking Ghost — Karen Finneyfrock

Clear Out the Static in Your Attic — Rebecca Bridge & Isla McKetta

Courage: Daring Poems for Gutsy Girls — Karen Finneyfrock, Mindy Nettifee
& Rachel McKibbens, Editors

Dear Future Boyfriend — Cristin O'Keefe Aptowicz

Dive: The Life and Fight of Reba Tutt — Hannah Safren

Drunks and Other Poems of Recovery — Jack McCarthy

The Elephant Engine High Dive Revival anthology

Everyone I Love Is A Stranger To Someone — Anneleyse Gelman

Everything Is Everything — Cristin O'Keefe Aptowicz

The Feather Room — Anis Mojgani

Floating, Brilliant, Gone — Franny Choi

Gentleman Practice — Buddy Wakefield

Glitter in the Blood: A Guide to Braver Writing — Mindy Nettifee

Good Grief — Stevie Edwards

The Good Things About America — Derrick Brown and Kevin Staniec, Editors

The Heart of a Comet — Pages D. Matam

Hot Teen Slut — Cristin O'Keefe Aptowicz

I Love Science! — Shanny Jean Maney

I Love You is Back — Derrick C. Brown

The Importance of Being Ernest — Ernest Cline

In Search of Midnight — Mike McGee

The Incredible Sestina Anthology — Daniel Nester, Editor

Junkyard Ghost Revival anthology

Kissing Oscar Wilde — Jade Sylvan

The Last Time as We Are — Taylor Mali

Learn Then Burn — Tim Stafford and Derrick C. Brown, Editors

Learn Then Burn Teacher's Manual — Tim Stafford and Molly Meacham, Editors

Learn Then Burn 2: This Time It's Personal — Tim Stafford, Editor

Live For A Living — Buddy Wakefield

Love in a Time of Robot Apocalypse — David Perez

The Madness Vase — Andrea Gibson

Multiverse: An anthology of Superhero Poetry of Superhuman Proportions —
Rob Sturma & Ryk Mcintyre

The New Clean — Jon Sands

New Shoes On A Dead Horse — Sierra DeMulder

No Matter the Wreckage — Sarah Kay

Oh, Terrible Youth — Cristin O'Keefe Aptowicz

The Oregon Trail Is The Oregon Trail — Gregory Sherl

Our Poison Horse — Derrick C. Brown

Over the Anvil We Stretch — Anis Mojgani

The Pocketknife Bible — Anis Mojgani

Pole Dancing to Gospel Hymns — Andrea Gibson

Racing Hummingbirds — Jeanann Verlee

Redhead and The Slaughter King — Megan Falley

Rise of the Trust Fall — Mindy Nettifee

Scandalabra — Derrick C. Brown

Slow Dance With Sasquatch — Jeremy Radin

The Smell of Good Mud — Lauren Zuniga

Songs from Under the River — Anis Mojgani

Spiking the Sucker Punch — Robbie Q. Telfer

CPSIA information can be obtained at www.ICGtesting.com
Printed in the USA
BVOW07s0536051114

373670BV00003B/5/P